THE BEST OF LED-ZEPPELIN VOL. 2

Published by
Wise Publications
14-15 Berners Street, London W1T 3LJ, UK

Exclusive Distributors:

Music Sales Limited
Distribution Centre, Newmarket Road,
Bury St Edmunds, Suffolk IP33 3YB, UK

Music Sales Pty Limited
20 Resolution Drive,
Caringbah, NSW 2229, Australia

Order No. AM996600
ISBN 978-1-84772-946-0
This book © Copyright 2010 Wise Publications,
a division of Music Sales Limited.

Unauthorised reproduction of any part of this
publication by any means including photocopying
is an infringement of copyright.

Cover designed by Liz Barrand
Photo research by Jacqui Black

Printed in the EU

www.musicsales.com

Your Guarantee of Quality
As publishers, we strive to produce every book
to the highest commercial standards.
The music has been freshly engraved and the book has
been carefully designed to minimise awkward page turns
and to make playing from it a real pleasure.
Particular care has been given to specifying acid-free,
neutral-sized paper made from pulps which have not been
elemental chlorine bleached. This pulp is from farmed
sustainable forests and was produced with special regard
for the environment.
Throughout, the printing and binding have been planned
to ensure a sturdy, attractive publication which should
give years of enjoyment.
If your copy fails to meet our high standards,
please inform us and we will gladly replace it.

www.musicsales.com

STAIRWAY TO HEAVEN 10

THE SONG REMAINS THE SAME 22

OVER THE HILLS AND FAR AWAY 36

TRAMPLED UNDER FOOT 44

KASHMIR 54

NOBODY'S FAULT BUT MINE 61

ACHILLES LAST STAND 72

ALL MY LOVE 94

GUITAR TABLATURE EXPLAINED 8

RECORDING NOTES

It is simply impossible to actually recreate the recorded performances of Led Zeppelin and the production techniques of Jimmy Page. The intention of these recordings is to aid study of the guitar parts by providing credible backing tracks to play-along with, hopefully capturing the spirit of the original music. Ultimately it is essential to listen to, and try and emulate the original Led Zeppelin tracks to really understand the musical nuance, intensity, and brilliance of those recordings.

CREDITS

Supervisory editors: Brad Tolinski and Jimmy Brown

Project manager and music editor: Tom Farncombe

Additional transcription and editing: Jimmy Brown, Dan Begelman and Jack Allen

Audio recorded and mixed by Jonas Persson

Guitars and guitar transcriptions: Arthur Dick
Bass guitar and bass transcriptions: Paul Townsend
Drums, percussion and drum transcriptions: Noam Lederman

Keyboards and keyboard transcriptions: Paul Honey

Recorders: Kirsten Halliday

Harmonica: Son Maxwell

'Kashmir' orchestra arrangement and programming: Rick Cardinali

With special thanks to Mark Lodge at Hiwatt UK for supplying the Hiwatt 100 Head – an exact replica of Jimmy Page's amp from the Led Zeppelin sessions.

Also thanks to Chandler guitars (www.chandlerguitars.co.uk).

Arthur Dick

Paul Townsend

Noam Lederman

EQUIPMENT LIST

In addition to the instruments specified below, the following were used for these recordings:

1968 Ludwig drum kit (24" bass drum; 13" rack tom; 16" floor tom; 18" second floor tom)
Ludwig 6.5x14" Supraphonic snare drum; Ludwig 8x14" Coliseum snare drum
Paiste cymbals

1991 'Longhorn' Fender Jazz bass
1978 Fender Precision bass
1962 reissue Fender Jazz bass (strung with flatwound strings)

Ashdown bass amplification

Nord Electro2 modelling keyboard

Miscellaneous Guitar effects:
Fulltone Full-Drive 2
Roger Mayer Treble Booster
Pete Cornish sustain pedal
Celmo Sardine Can compressor
Jim Dunlop Crybaby Wah-wah

1968 Ludwig drum kit

The following notes detail the guitars and amplifiers used on each song, as an indication of how one might try to match the kind of tone Jimmy Page achieved on the original Led Zeppelin recordings. These were chosen according to the information available about the original recording set-ups; however, with other less-controllable factors to consider (studio size, mic type and placement, location, tape machines and recording consoles, for example), choices about the right sound were driven as much by ear as the reported original conditions.

STAIRWAY TO HEAVEN

The acoustic parts for this song were performed on a Santa Cruz Model D guitar; this was recorded with U47 Neumann and Sennheiser 421 microphones alongside two AKG 414 ambient mics.

The electric parts were played on a 1969 Fender Telecaster through a 1965 VOX AC30 and a Fender XII 12-string through a 10-watt Cornell Romany amplifier.

All the solo parts were played on the '69 Telecaster through a Marshall JCM2000 with a 4x12 cab.

The keyboard parts were played on the Nord Electro2 Fender Rhodes patch.

THE SONG REMAINS THE SAME

The 12-string parts on this song were recorded with a Rickenbacker 12 through the Marshall. The other electric parts were tracked with a 1952 Gibson Les Paul and a 1964 Epiphone Casino, both through the 1965 VOX AC30.

The solos were played on the 1969 Telecaster through the Cornell.

OVER THE HILLS AND FAR AWAY

The acoustic parts for this are a combination of a Santa Cruz 'D' 6-string and a Brook 12-string.

The electric parts were played on the 1952 Les Paul through a Hiwatt 100 amp.

The solo sound was achieved with a 1959 Les Paul, with the signal split between a direct input – rectified with a Tubetech valve compressor – and the VOX AC30, recorded using a combination of close and ambient microphones, with automated panning and Eventide Instant Phaser effects.

KASHMIR

The main guitar for this was a 1965 Danelectro Model CD 59 (courtesy of Dave Cousins from the Strawbs) recorded through the VOX AC30.

The other parts used the 1969 Telecaster and the Marshall.

TRAMPLED UNDER FOOT

All the guitar parts for this song were recorded using the 1959 Les Paul and the Hiwatt. The lead parts in the second and third verses have an automated reverse reverb effect created in Pro Tools.

The Keyboard parts are on a Nord Electro2 clavinet recorded through the 1965 Vox AC30.

ACHILLES LAST STAND

The main verse guitars for 'Achilles Last Stand' were created with a 1959 Les Paul and the Hiwatt; the other guitars were recorded on the 1952 Les Paul, again through the Hiwatt. The tremolo effects are from the Roger Mayer Voodoo Vibe+ pedal.

In the last 5/4 section the high guitar was pitchshifted by an octave to achieve the octave effects.

NOBODY'S FAULT BUT MINE

The intro riffs were tracked on the 1959 Les Paul, through the Hiwatt, and the '52 Les Paul through the Hiwatt and Cornell. The octave part is on the same guitar with an Eventide Instant Phaser.

The solo was played on the 1969 Telecaster through the Hiwatt and Cornell.

The harmonica solo was recorded through the VOX AC30.

ALL MY LOVE

The acoustic parts for this were played on a Santa Cruz Model D. The original recording featured a Telecaster fitted with a B-bender; this was emulated on a standard 1969 Telecaster through the Hiwatt.

The nylon-string parts were played on an Edward B. Jones Oxford classical guitar.

The electric parts were recorded on a 1969 Telecaster through the Marshall JCM2000.

The keyboard sounds are synth strings and 'trumpet' patches from the Expand sampler in Pro Tools.

Guitar Tablature Explained

Guitar music can be notated in three different ways: on a musical stave, in tablature, and in rhythm slashes.

RHYTHM SLASHES: are written above the stave. Strum chords in the rhythm indicated. Round noteheads indicate single notes.

THE MUSICAL STAVE: shows pitches and rhythms and is divided by lines into bars. Pitches are named after the first seven letters of the alphabet.

TABLATURE: graphically represents the guitar fingerboard. Each horizontal line represents a string, and each number represents a fret.

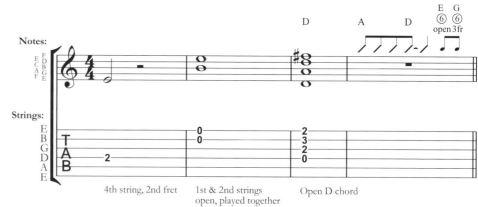

Definitions for Special Guitar Notation

SEMI-TONE BEND: Strike the note and bend up a semi-tone (½ step).

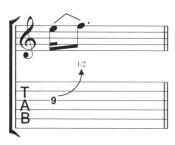

WHOLE-TONE BEND: Strike the note and bend up a whole-tone (full step).

GRACE NOTE BEND: Strike the note and bend as indicated. Play the first note as quickly as possible.

QUARTER-TONE BEND: Strike the note and bend up a ¼ step.

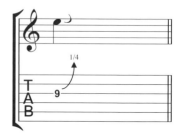

BEND & RELEASE: Strike the note and bend up as indicated, then release back to the original note.

COMPOUND BEND & RELEASE: Strike the note and bend up and down in the rhythm indicated.

PRE-BEND: Bend the note as indicated, then strike it.

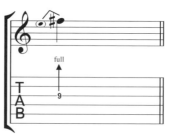

PRE-BEND & RELEASE: Bend the note as indicated. Strike it and release the note back to the original pitch.

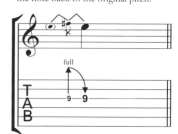

HAMMER-ON: Strike the first note with one finger, then sound the second note (on the same string) with another finger by fretting it without picking.

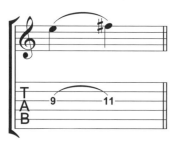

PULL-OFF: Place both fingers on the note to be sounded, strike the first note and without picking, pull the finger off to sound the second note.

LEGATO SLIDE (GLISS): Strike the first note and then slide the same fret-hand finger up or down to the second note. The second note is not struck.

MUFFLED STRINGS: A percussive sound is produced by laying the first hand across the string(s) without depressing, and striking them with the pick hand.

NATURAL HARMONIC: Strike the note while the fret-hand lightly touches the string directly over the fret indicated.

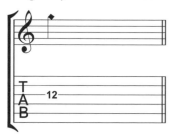

PICK SCRAPE: The edge of the pick is rubbed down (or up) the string, producing a scratchy sound.

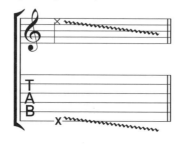

PALM MUTING: The note is partially muted by the pick hand lightly touching the string(s) just before the bridge.

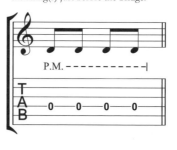

SHIFT SLIDE (GLISS & RESTRIKE): Same as legato slide, except the second note is struck.

TAP HARMONIC: The note is fretted normally and a harmonic is produced by tapping or slapping the fret indicated in brackets (which will be twelve frets higher than the fretted note.)

TAPPING: Hammer ('tap') the fret indicated with the pick-hand index or middle finger and pull-off to the note fretted by the fret hand.

PINCH HARMONIC: The note is fretted normally and a harmonic is produced by adding the edge of the thumb or the tip of the index finger of the pick hand to the normal pick attack.

ARTIFICIAL HARMONIC: The note is fretted normally and a harmonic is produced by gently resting the pick hand's index finger directly above the indicated fret (in brackets) while plucking the appropriate string.

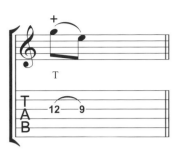
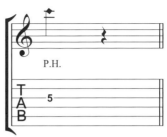
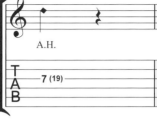

TRILL: Very rapidly alternate between the notes indicated by continuously hammering-on and pulling-off.

RAKE: Drag the pick across the strings with a single motion.

TREMOLO PICKING: The note is picked as rapidly and continuously as possible.

ARPEGGIATE: Play the notes of the chord indicated by quickly rolling them from bottom to top.

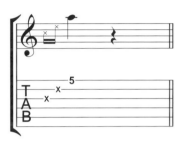

SWEEP PICKING: Rhythmic downstroke and/or upstroke motion across the strings.

VIBRATO DIVE BAR AND RETURN: The pitch of the note or chord is dropped a specific number of steps (in rhythm) then returned to the original pitch.

VIBRATO BAR SCOOP: Depress the bar just before striking the note, then quickly release the bar.

VIBRATO BAR DIP: Strike the note and then immediately drop a specific number of steps, then release back to the original pitch.

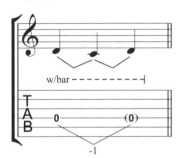

ADDITIONAL MUSICAL DEFINITIONS

 (accent)   Accentuate note (play it louder)   **D.S. al Coda**   Go back to the sign (𝄋), then play until the bar marked **To Coda** ✛ then skip to the section marked ✛ **Coda**

 (accent)   Accentuate note with greater intensity   **D.C. al Fine**   Go back to the beginning of the song and play until the bar marked **Fine.**

 (staccato)   Shorten time value of note   tacet   Instrument is silent (drops out).

⊓   Downstroke

V   Upstroke      Repeat bars between signs

NOTE: Tablature numbers in brackets mean:
1. The note is sustained, but a new articulation (such as hammer-on or slide) begins
2. A note may be fretted but not necessarily played.

When a repeat section has different endings, play the first ending only the first time and the second ending only the second time.

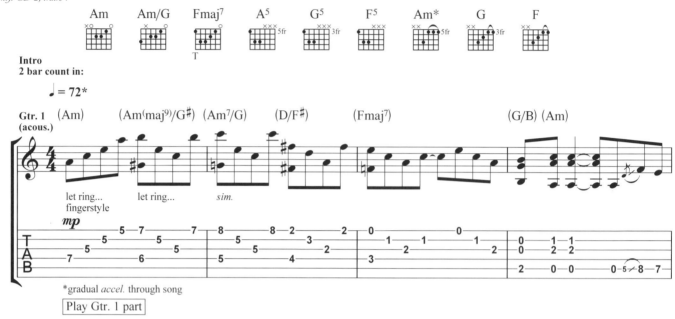
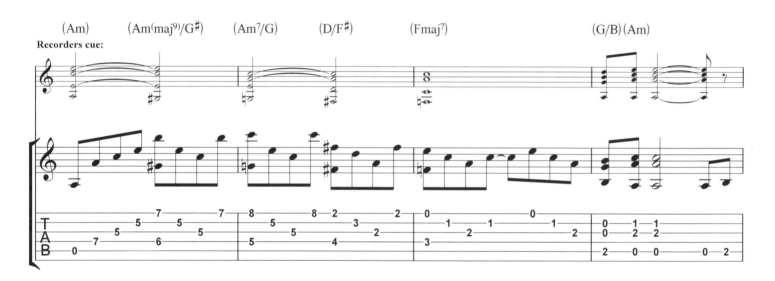
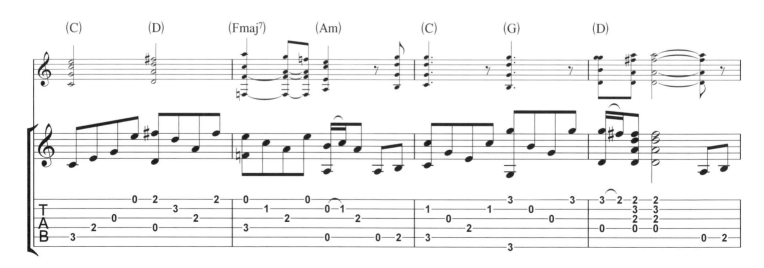

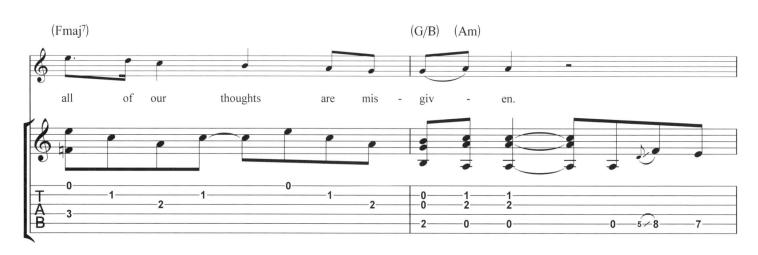

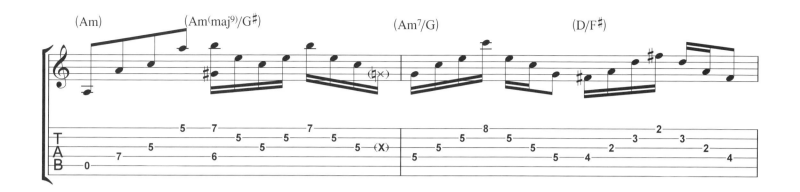
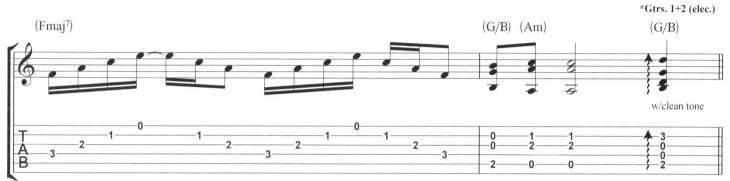
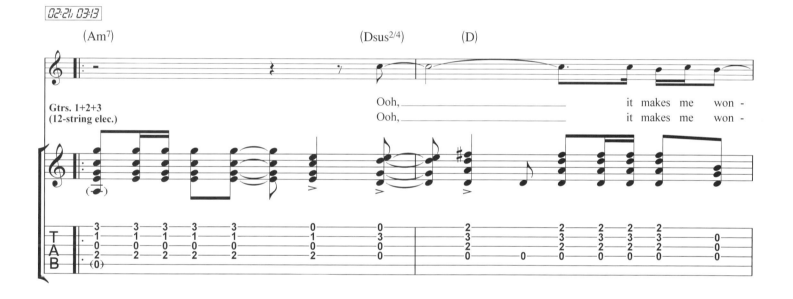
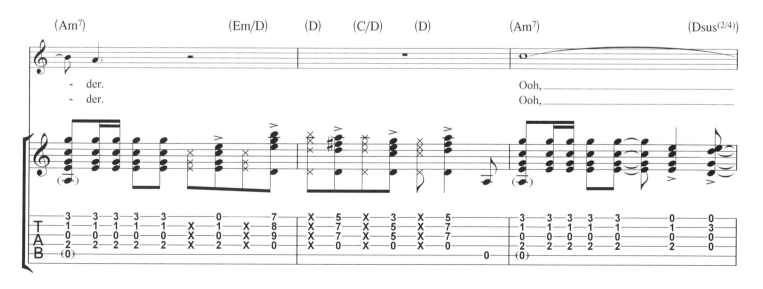

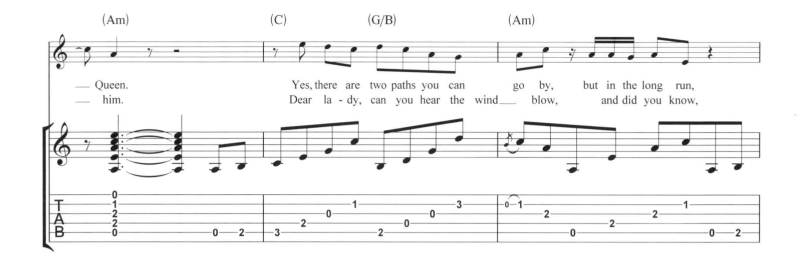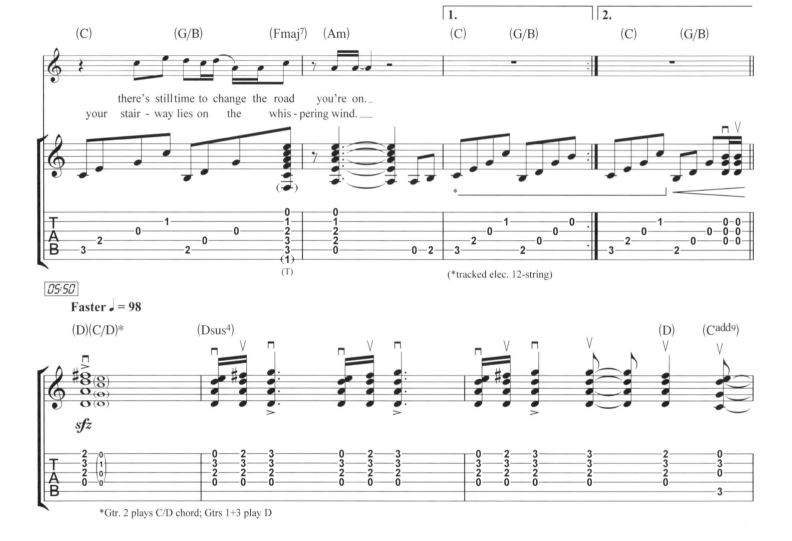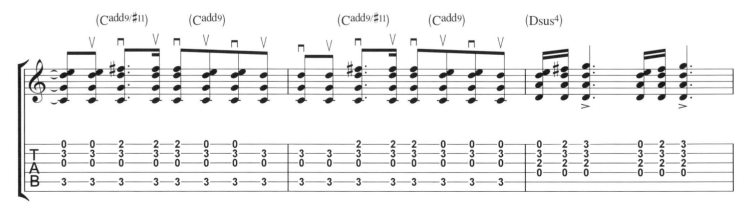

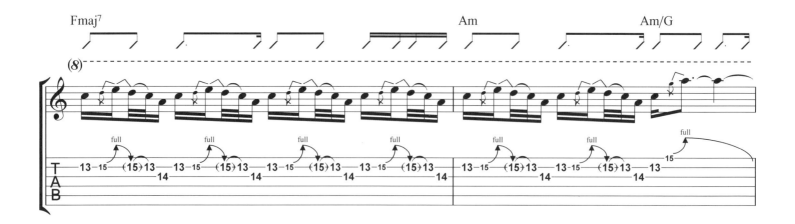
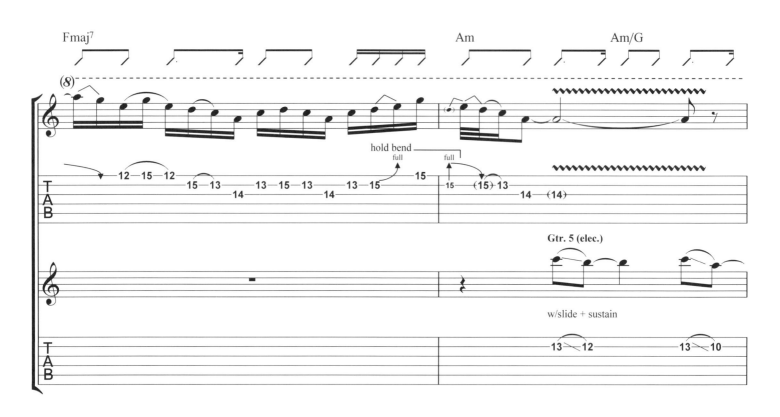
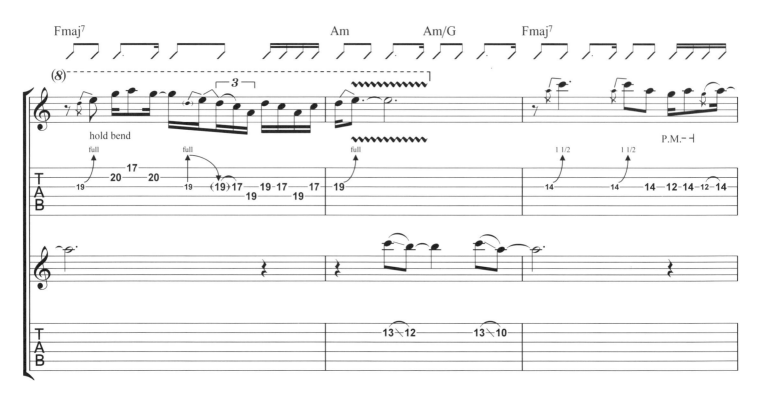

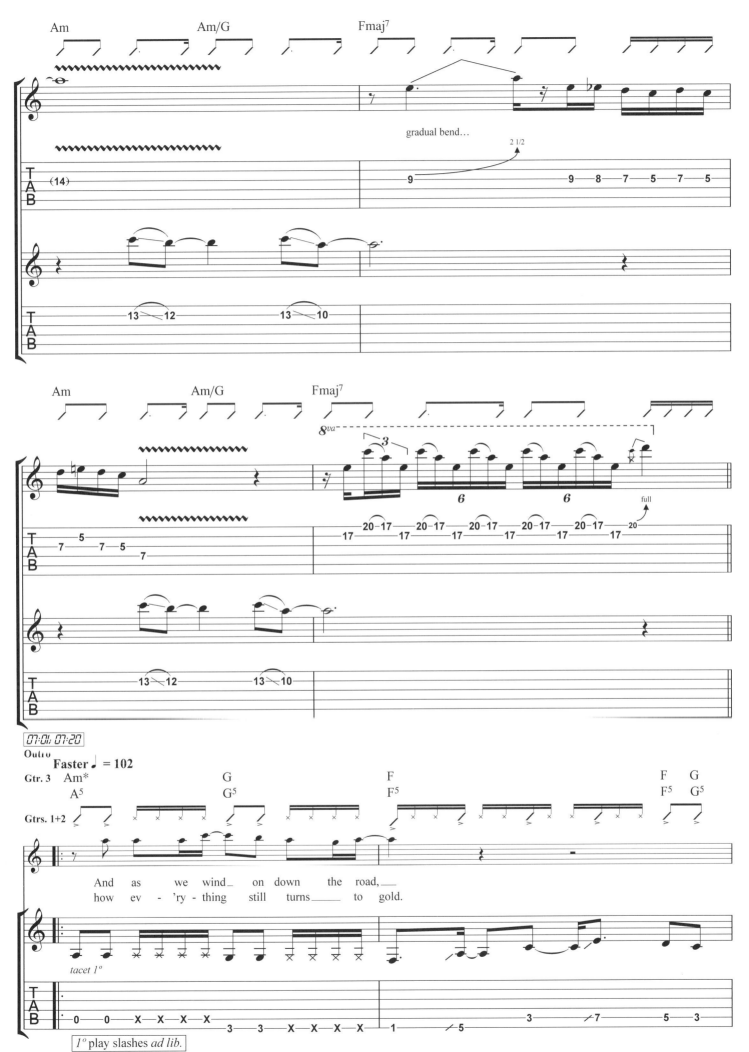

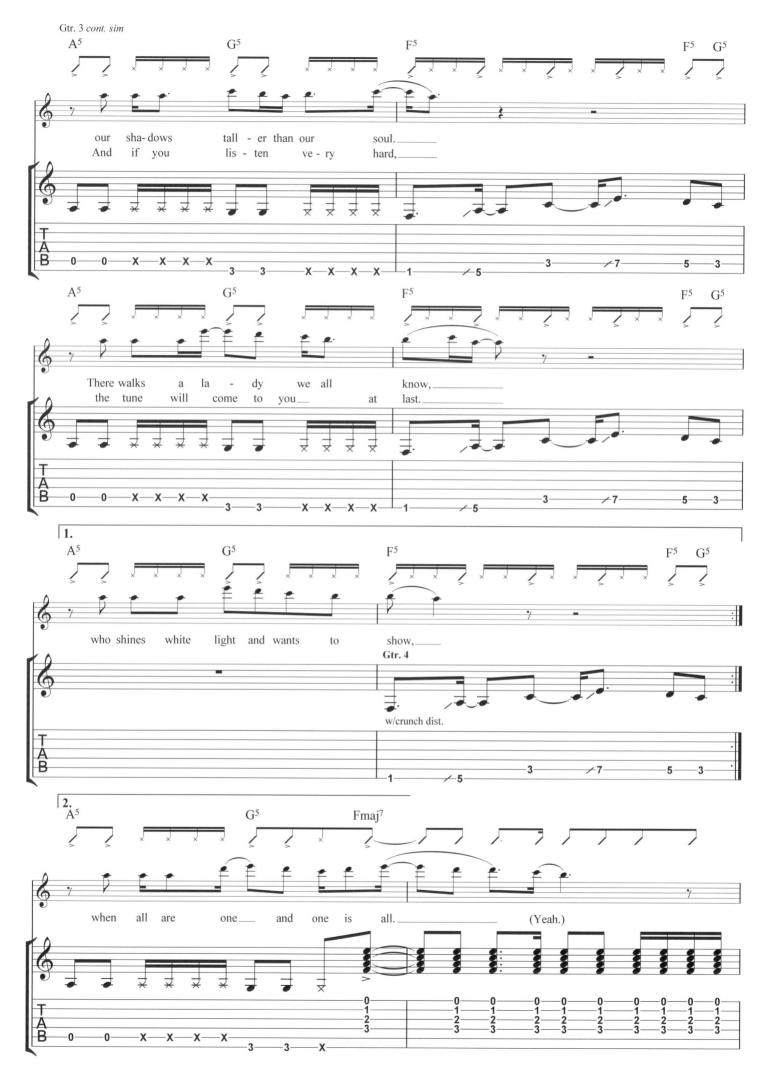

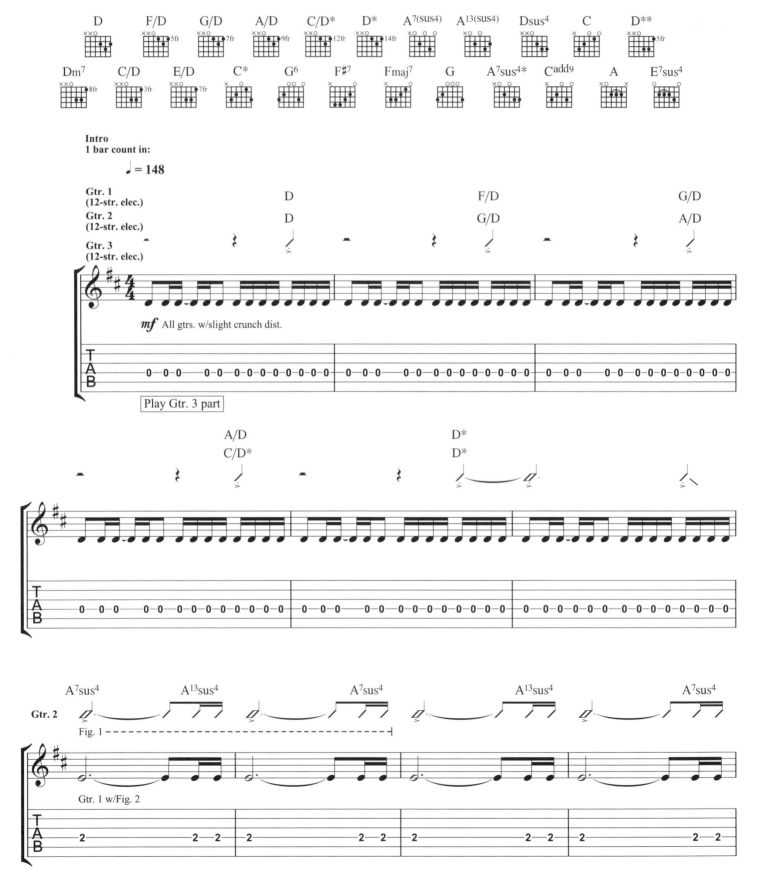

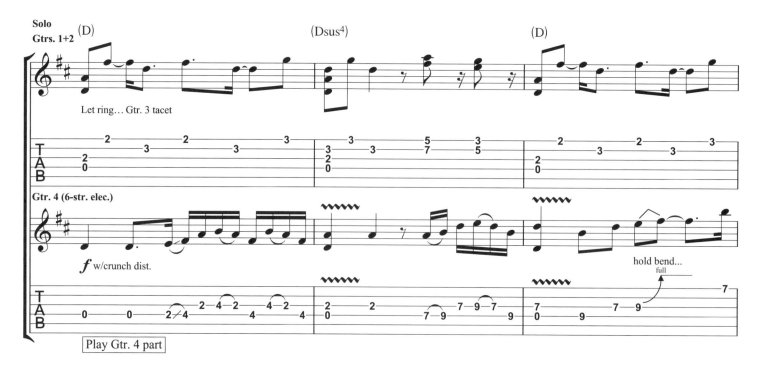

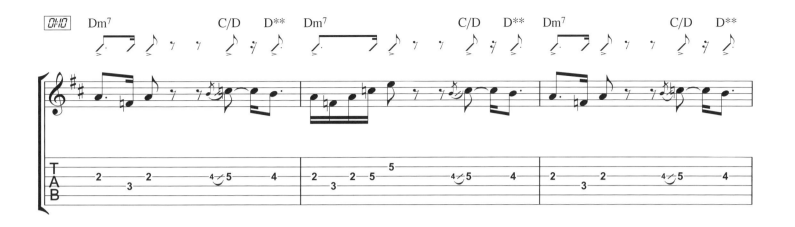
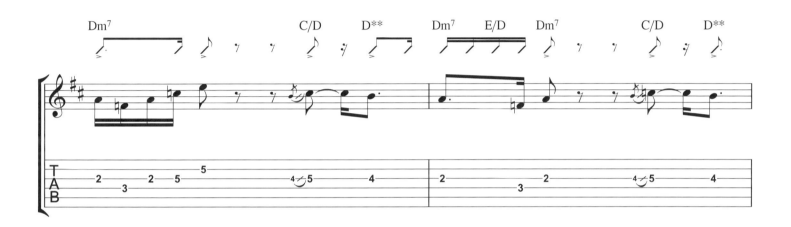
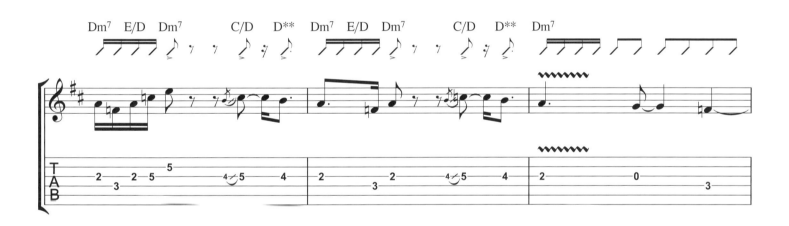
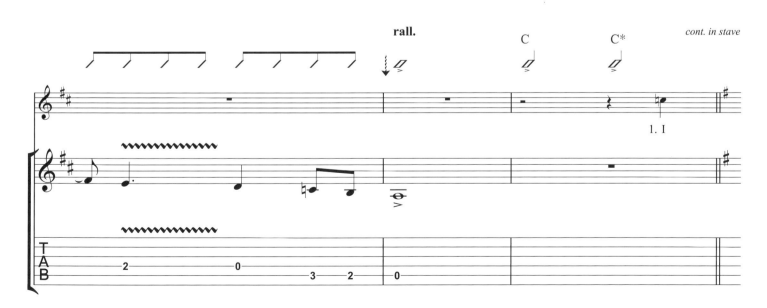

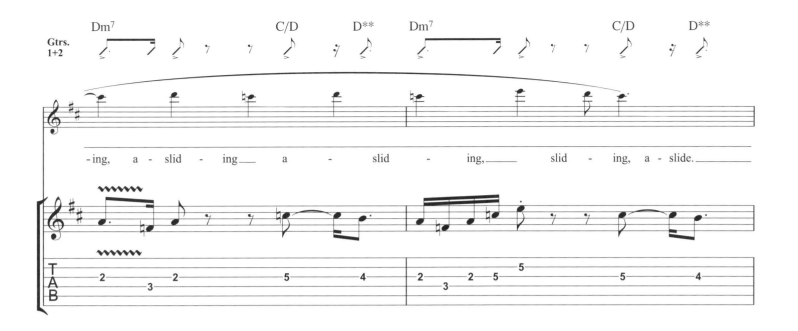
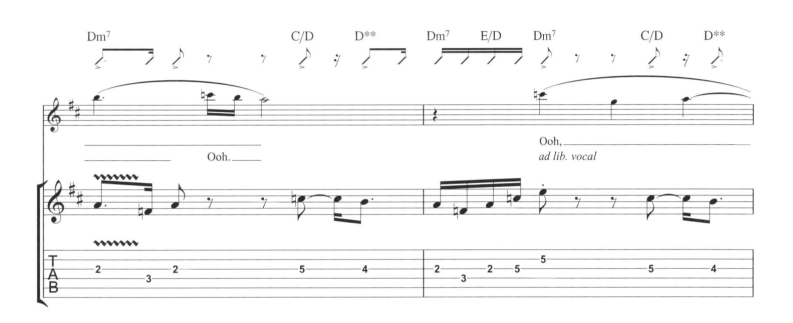
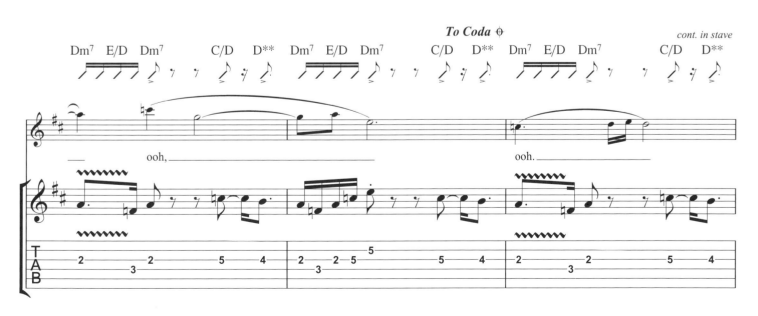

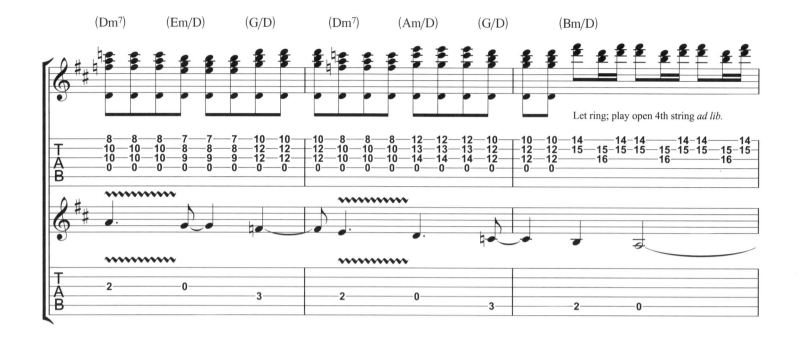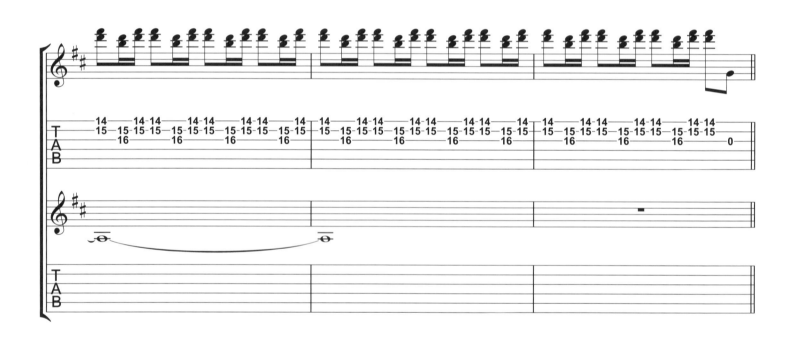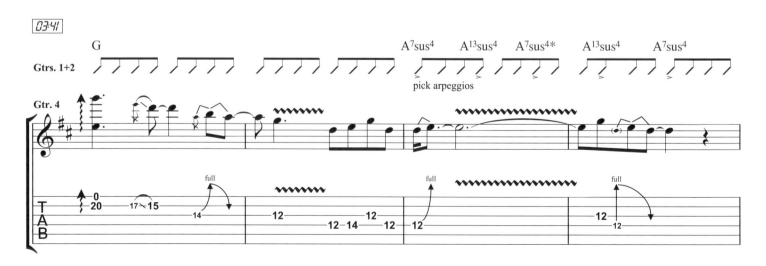

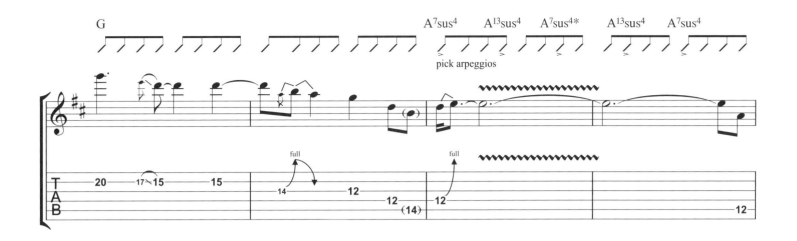
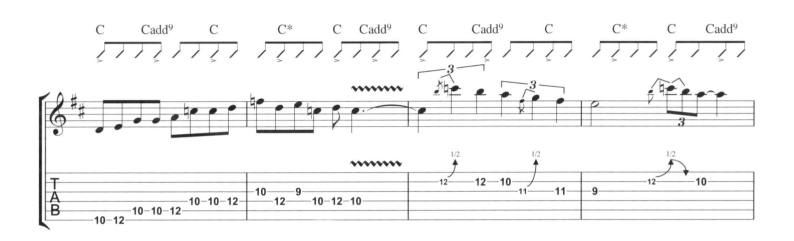
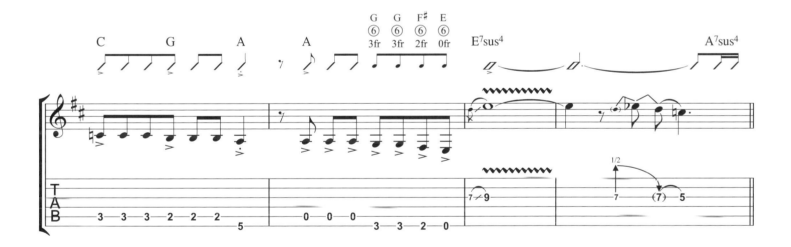
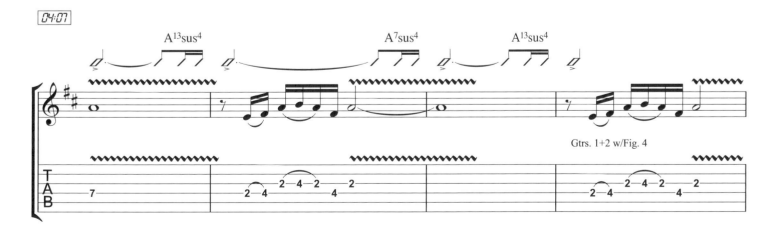

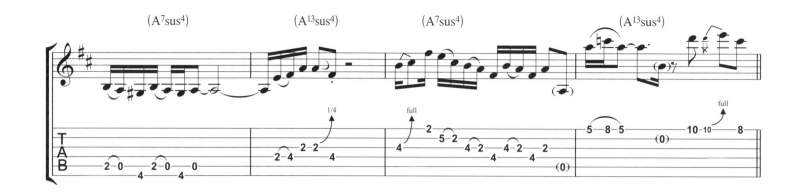
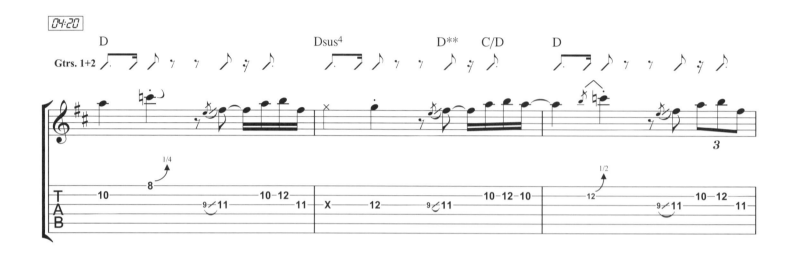
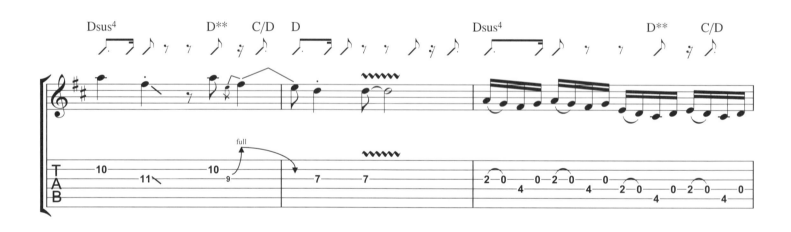

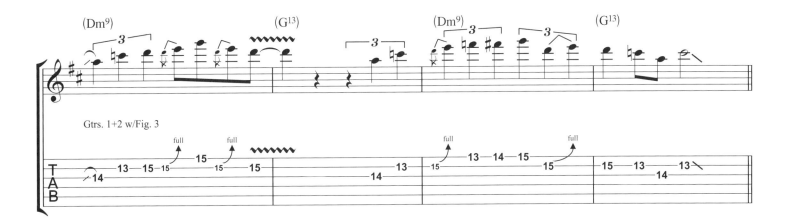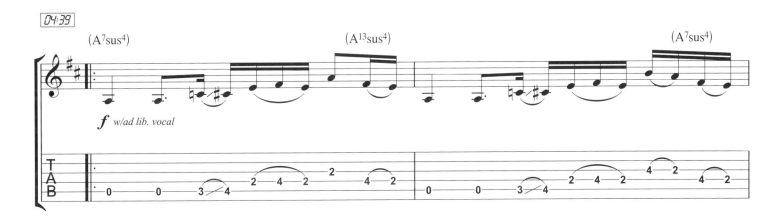

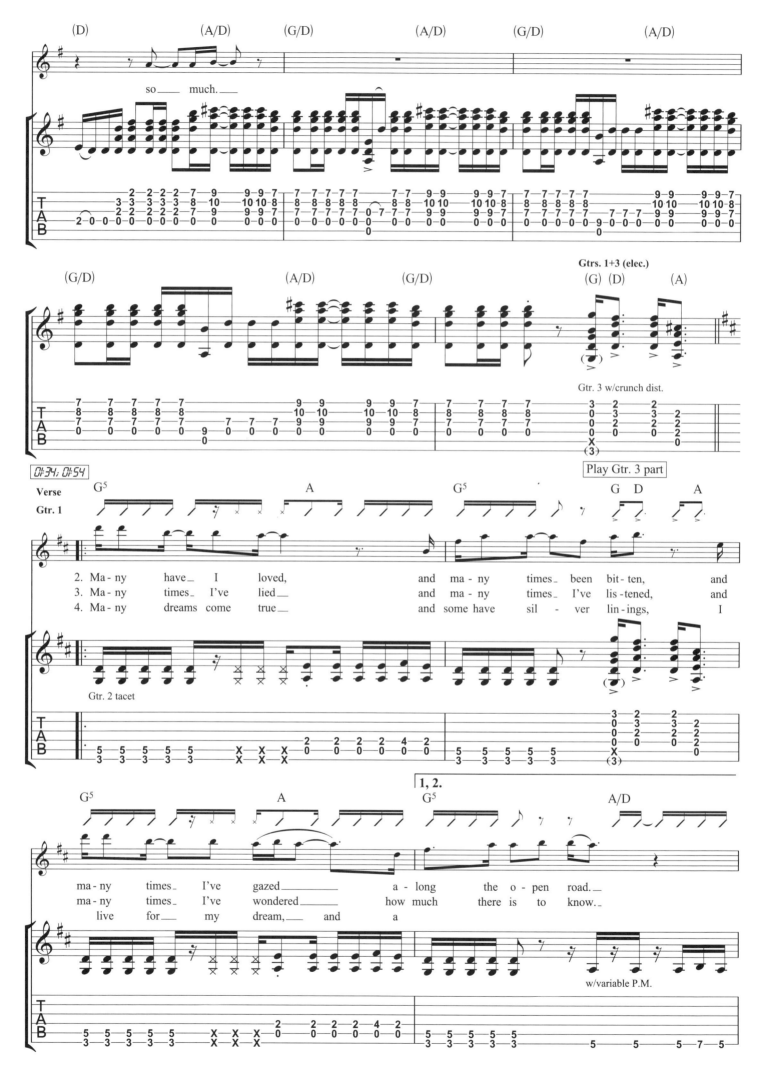

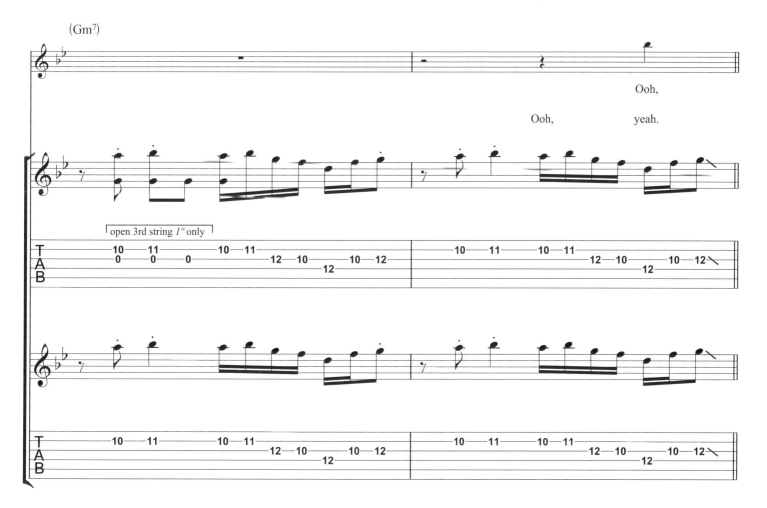

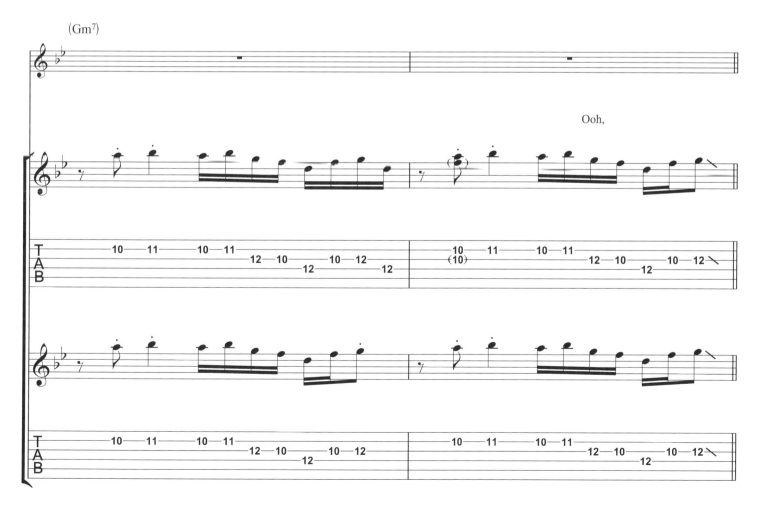

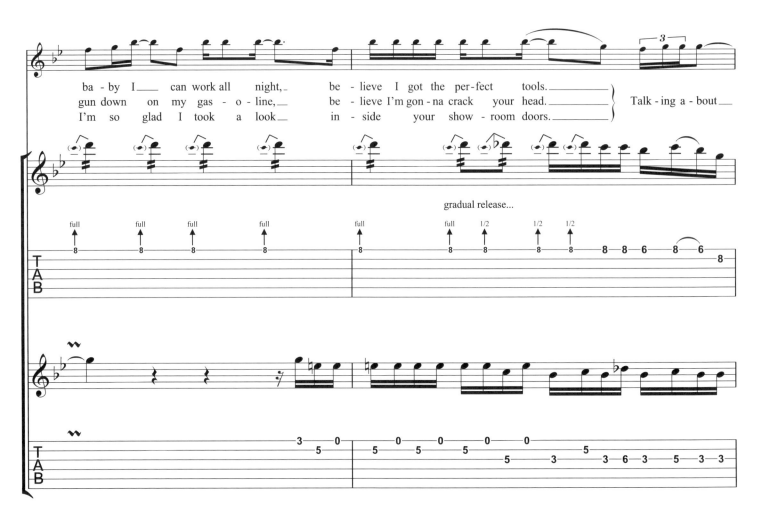

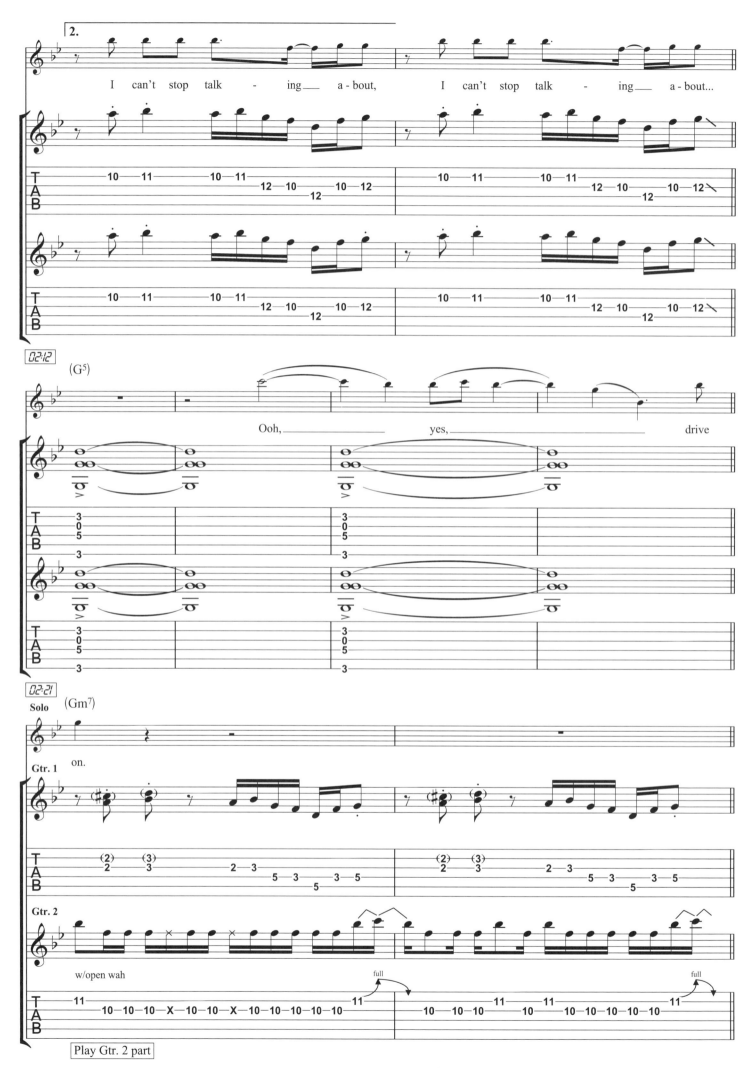

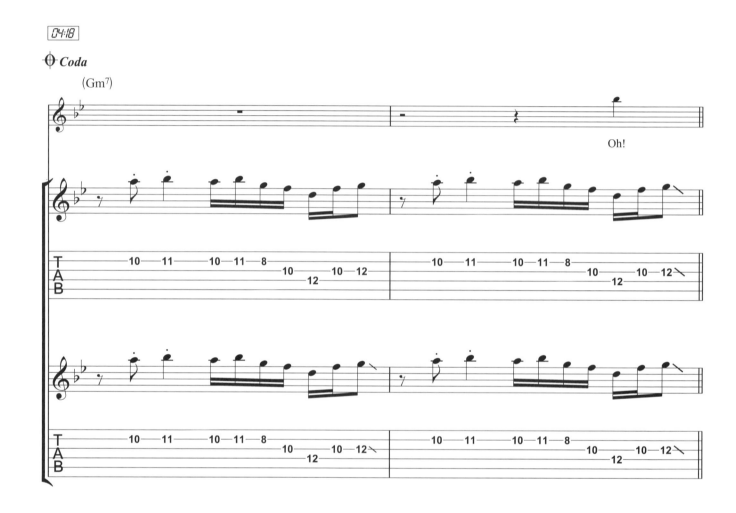

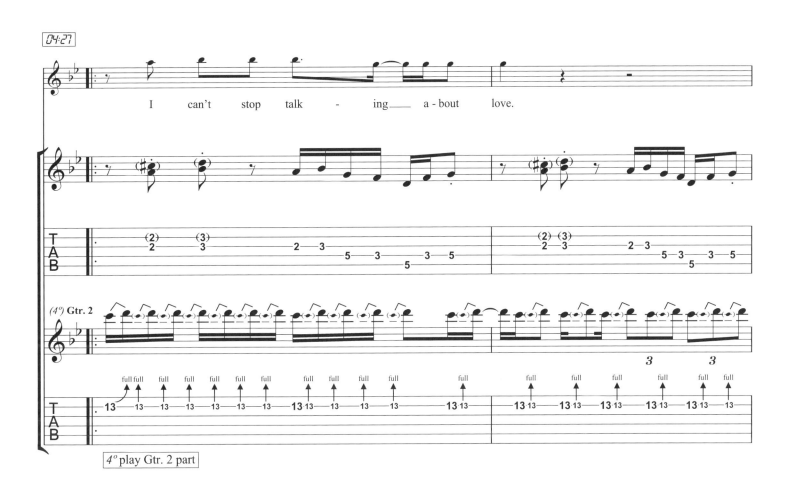
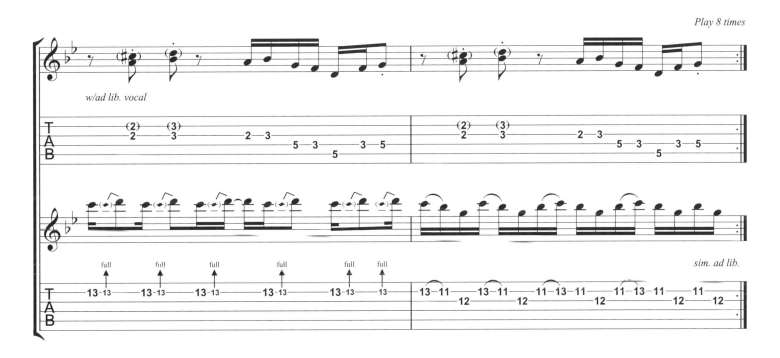

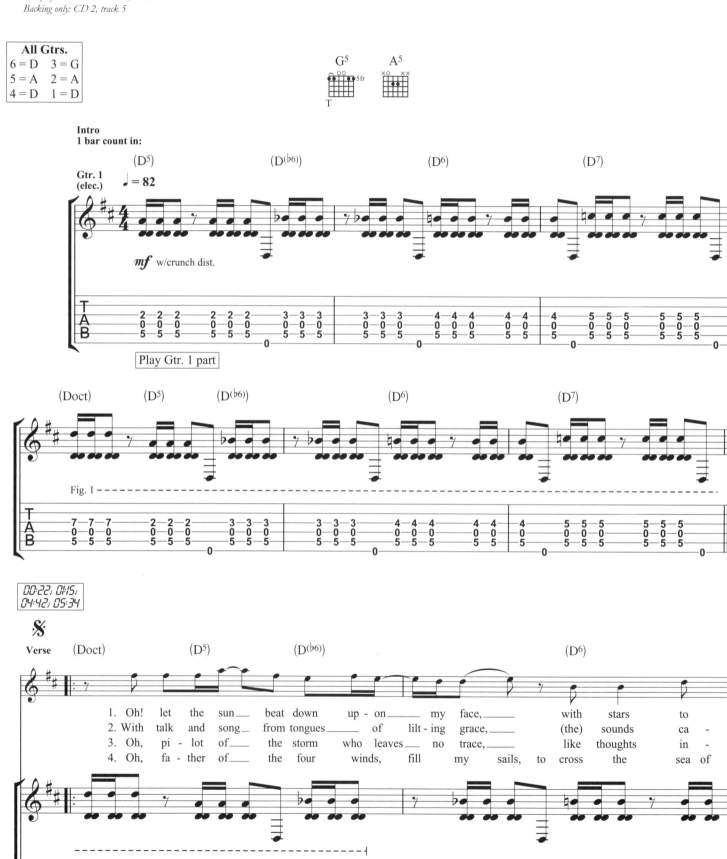

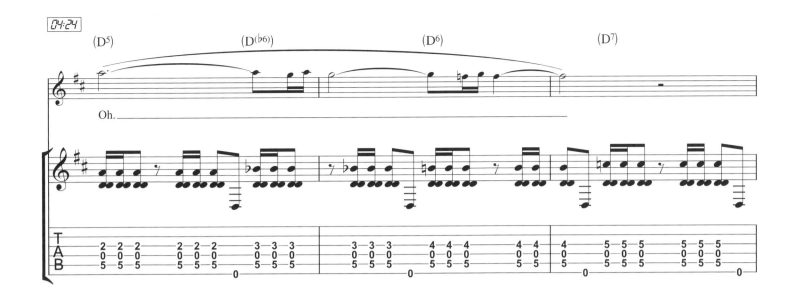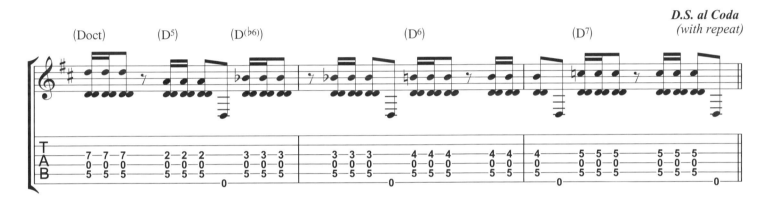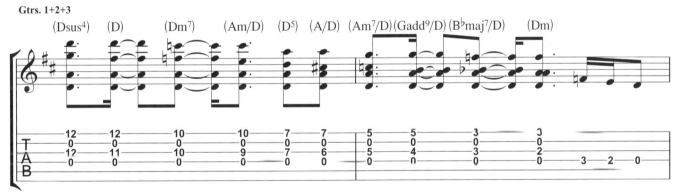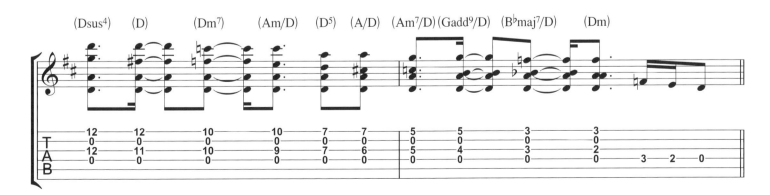

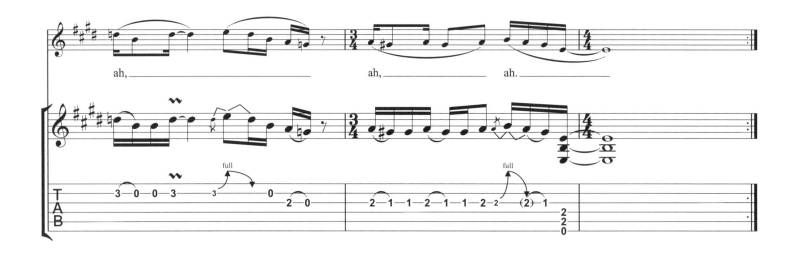
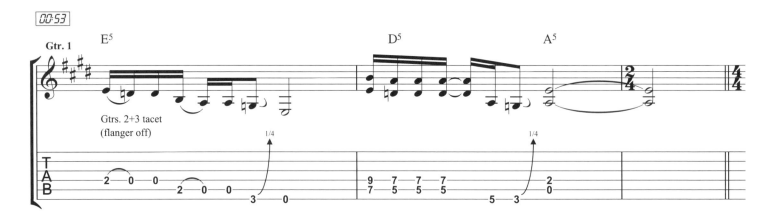
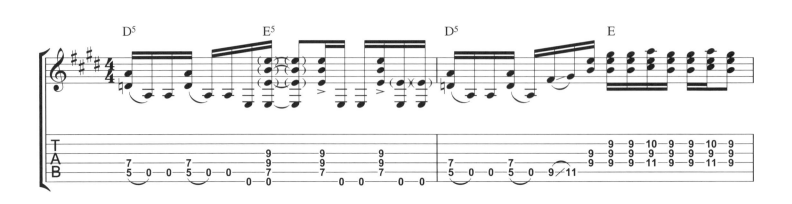
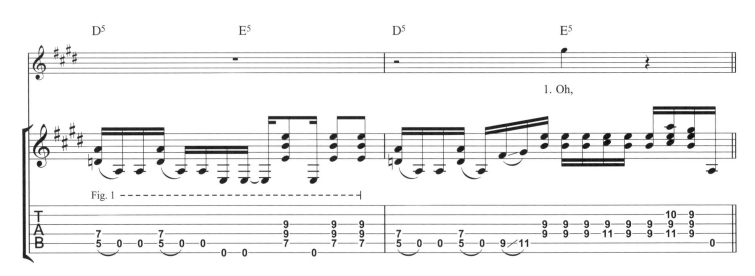

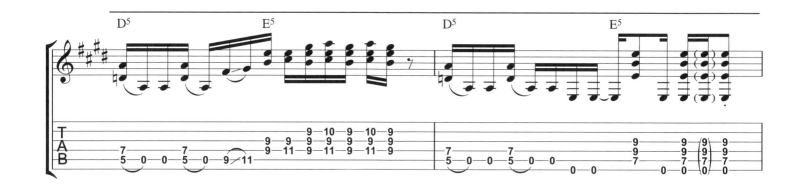
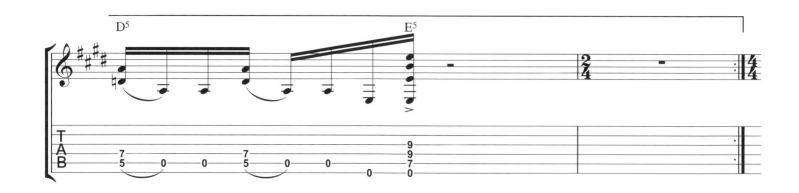
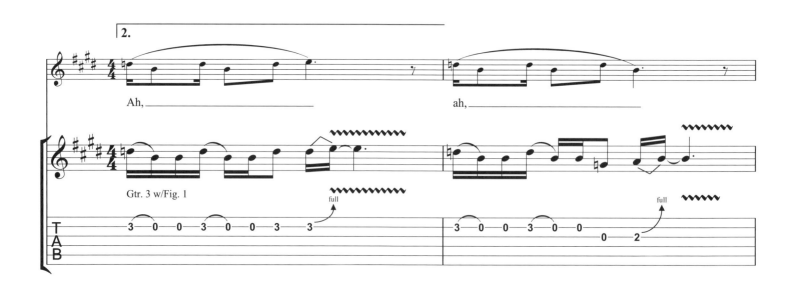

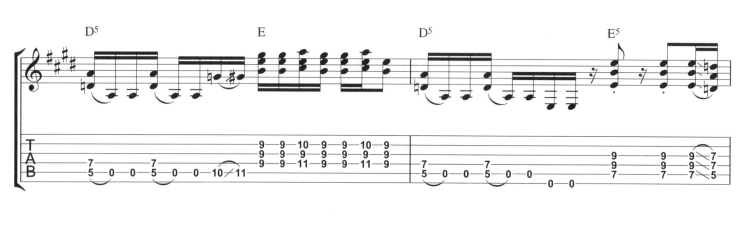
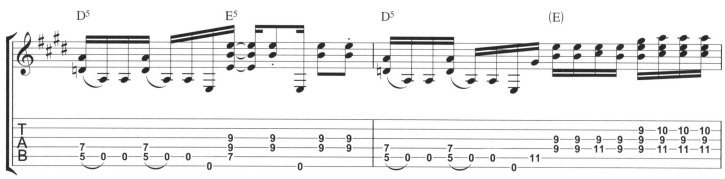
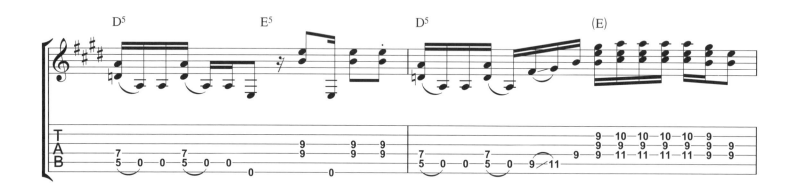
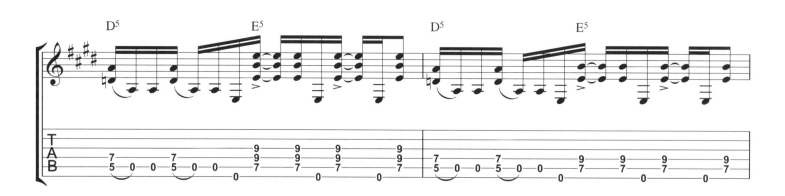
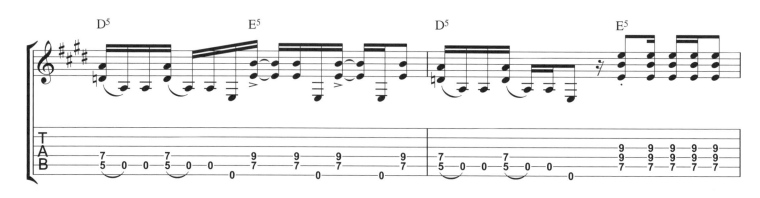

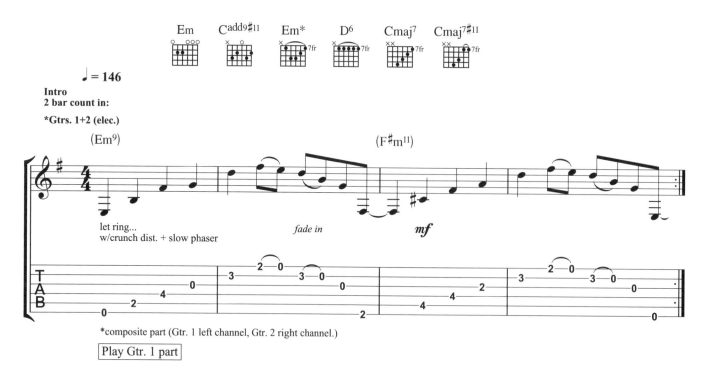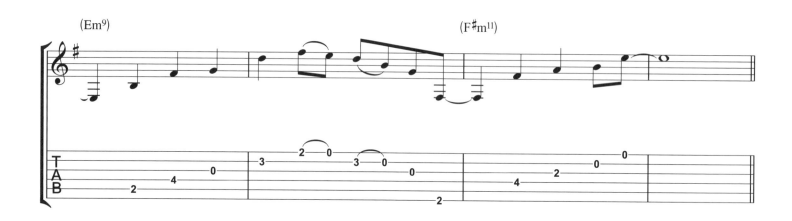

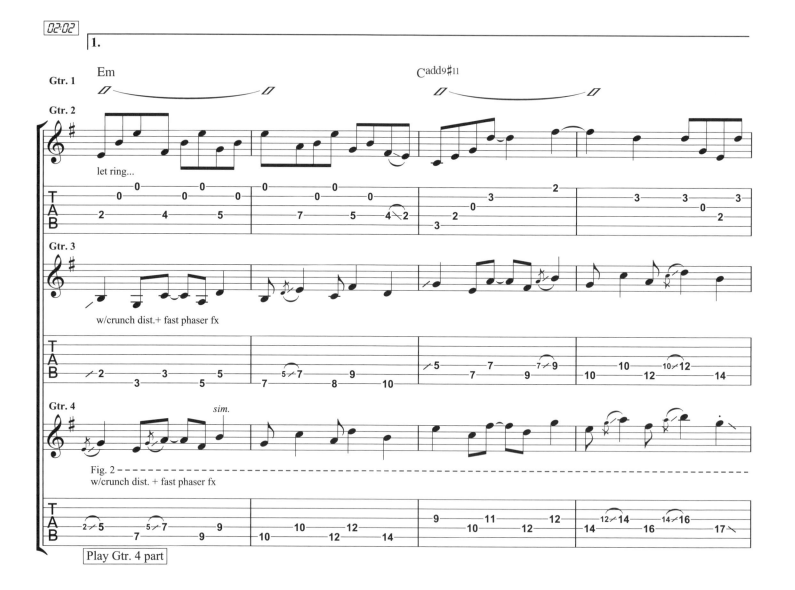

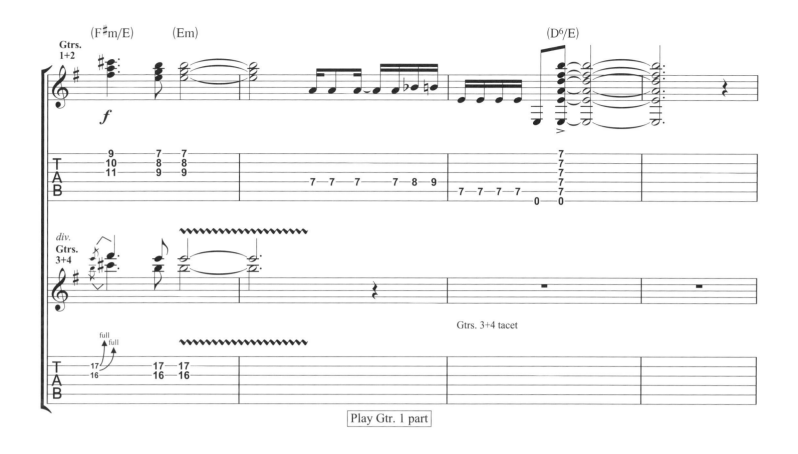

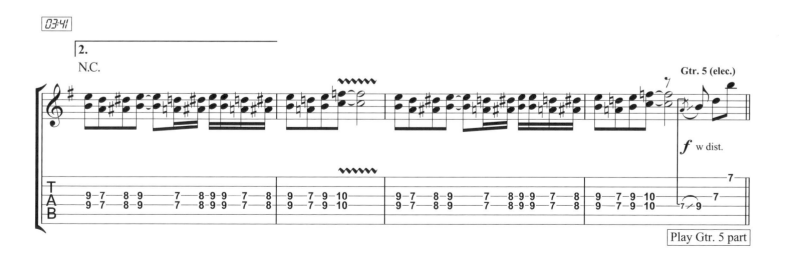

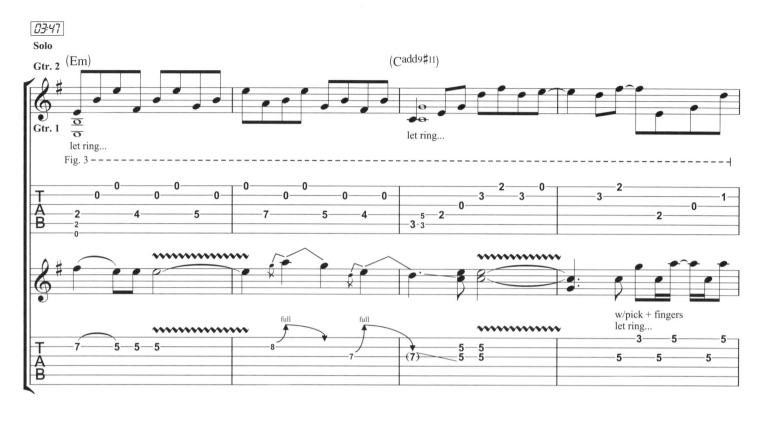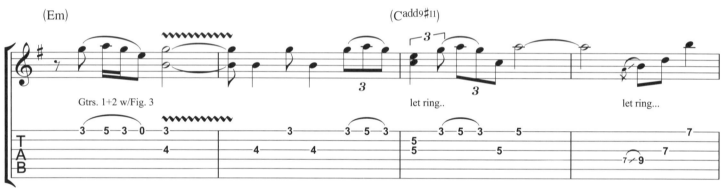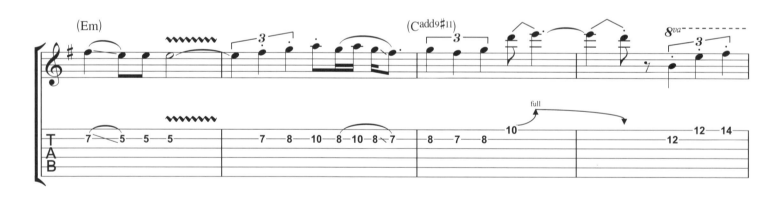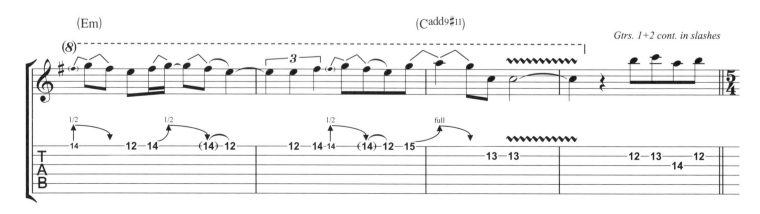

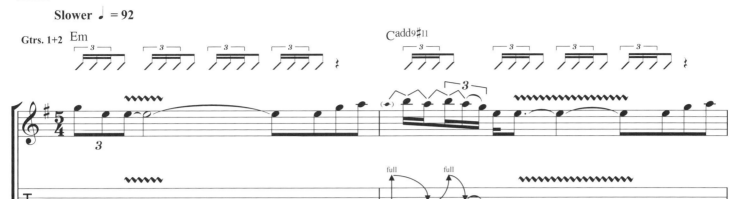
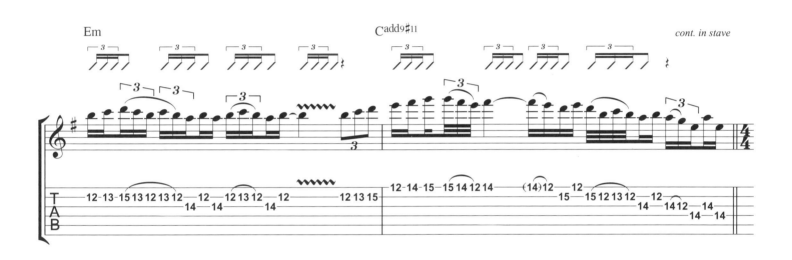
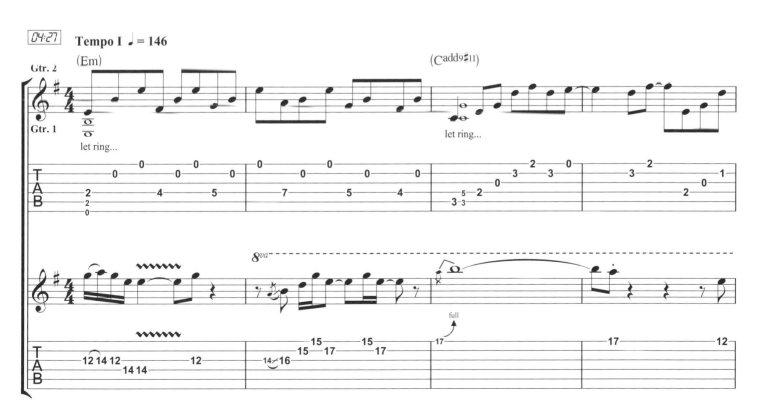

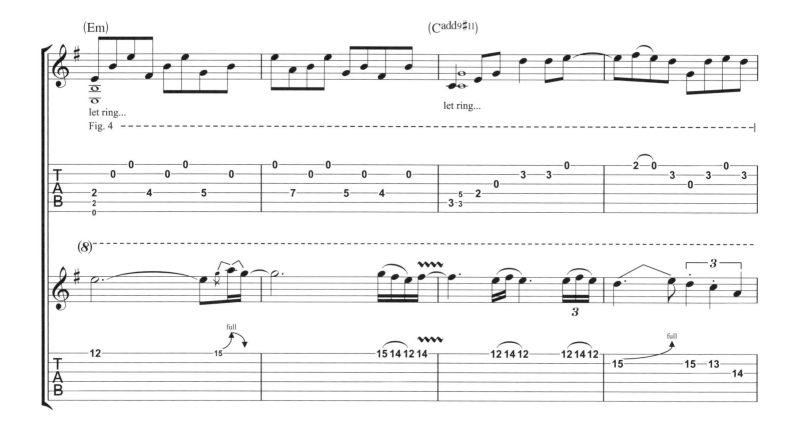
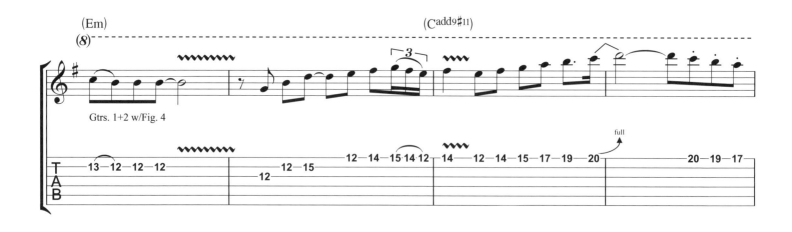
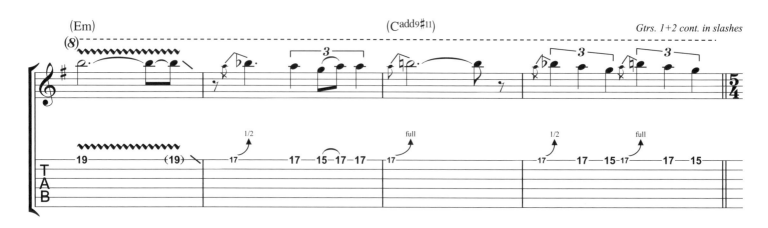

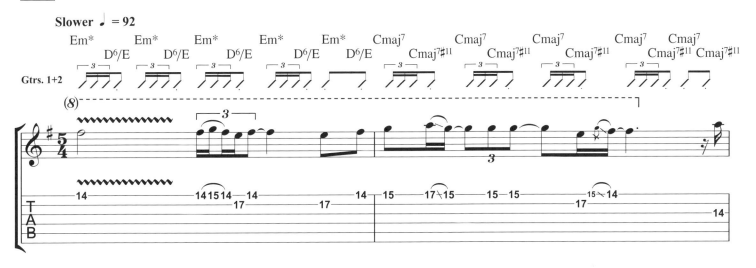
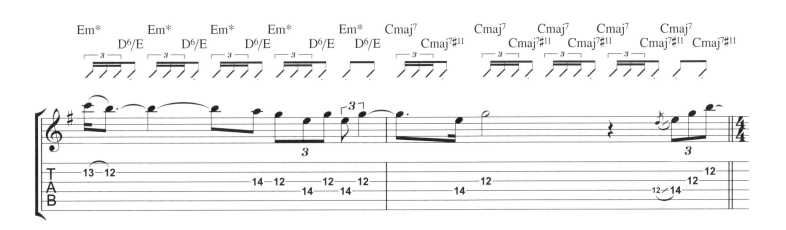
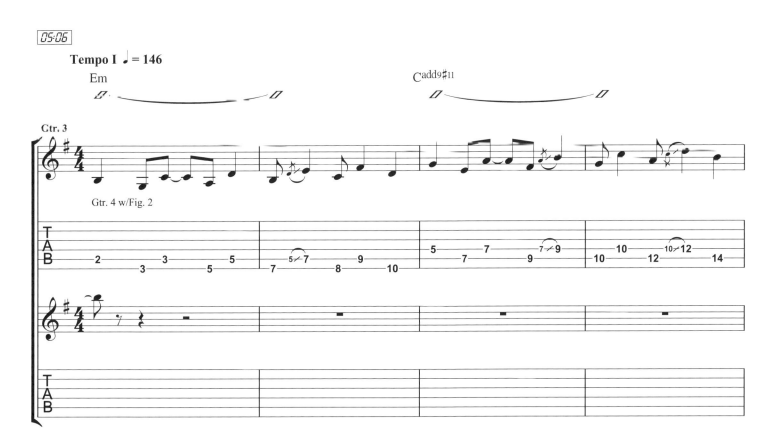

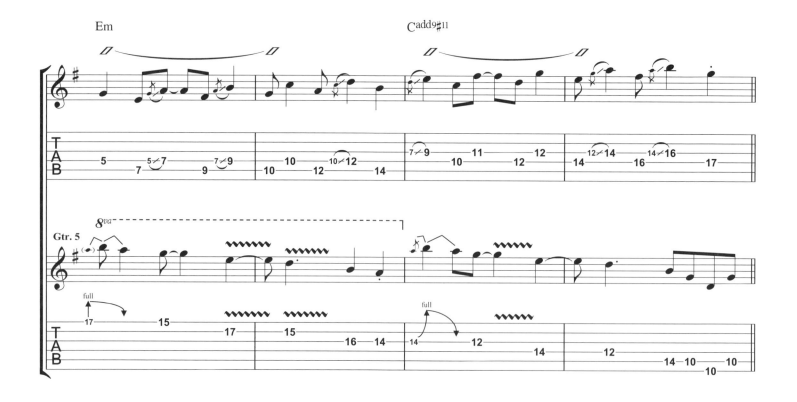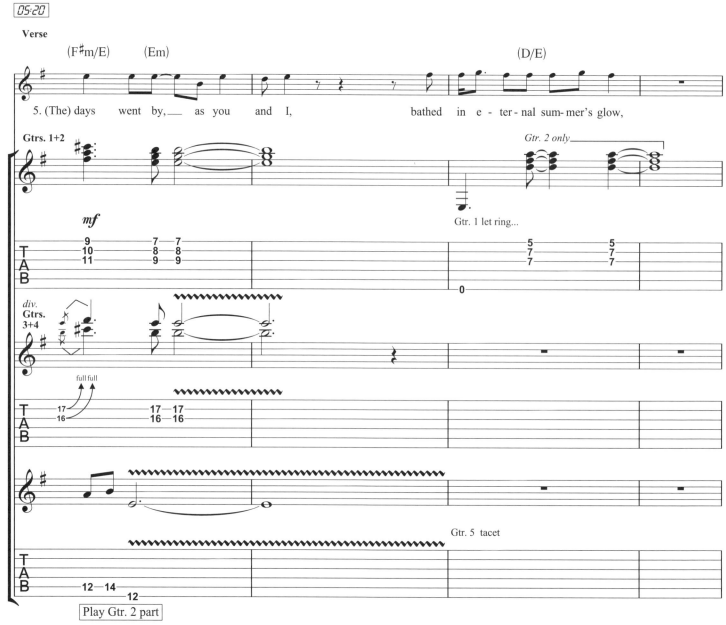

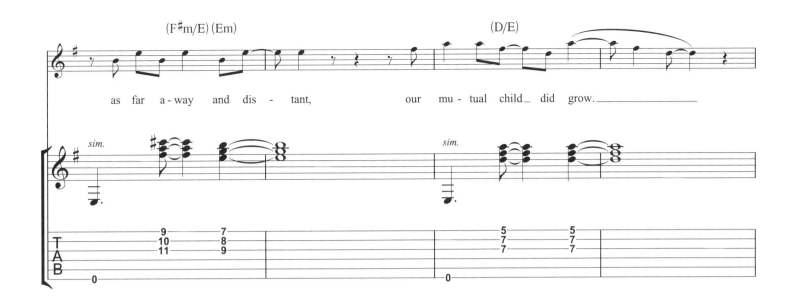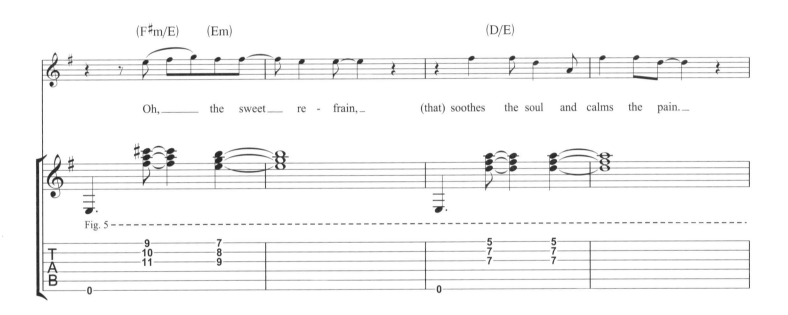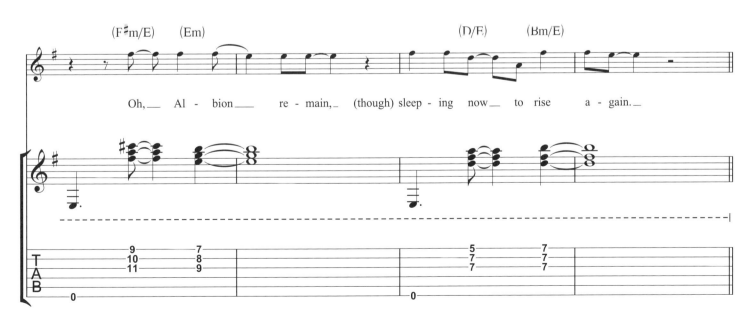

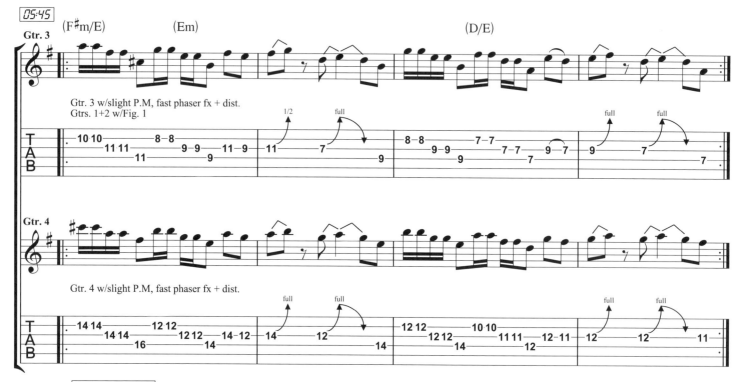
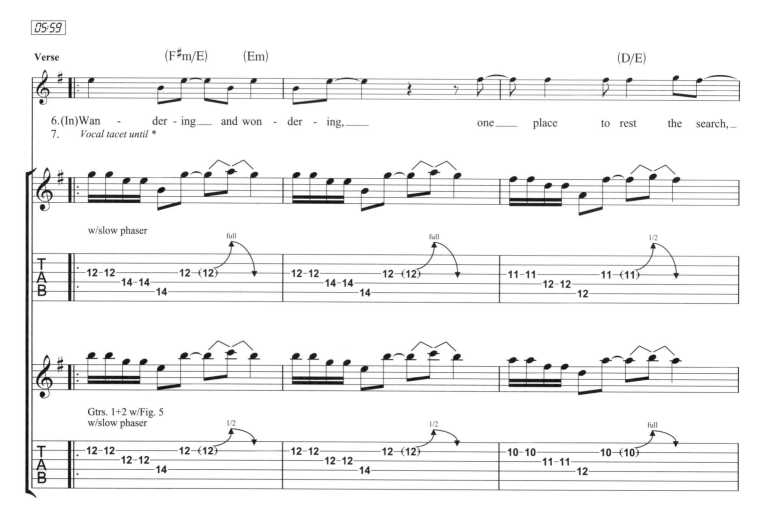

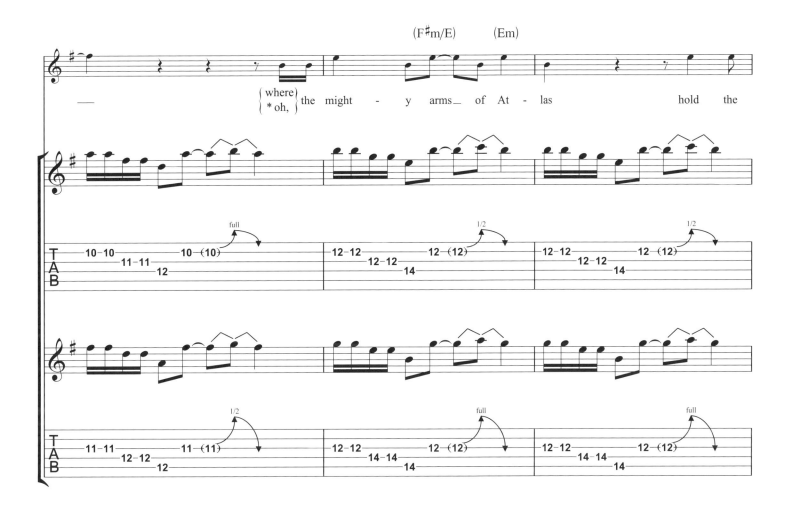
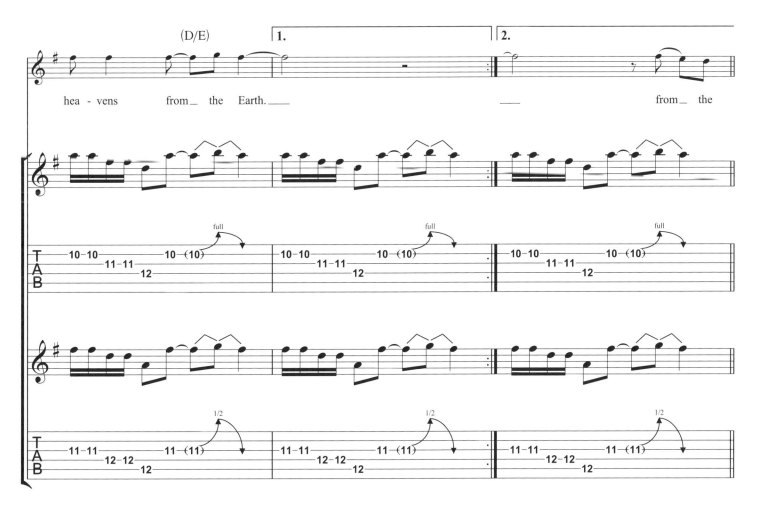

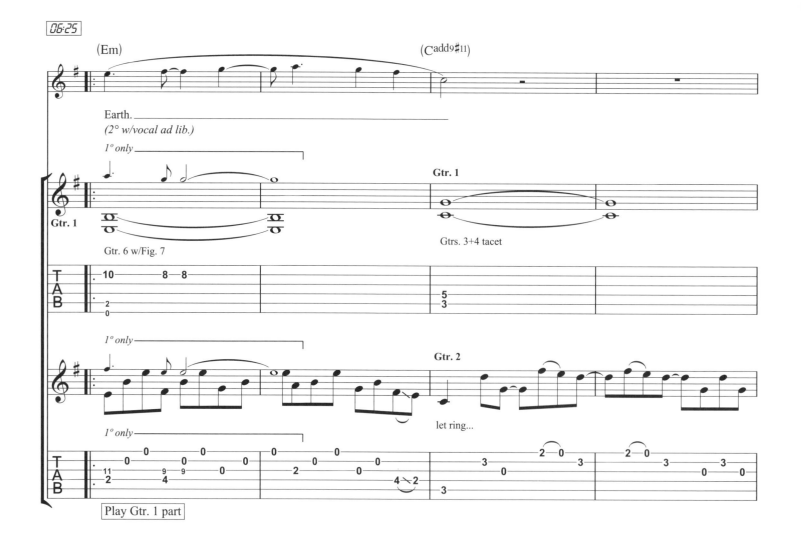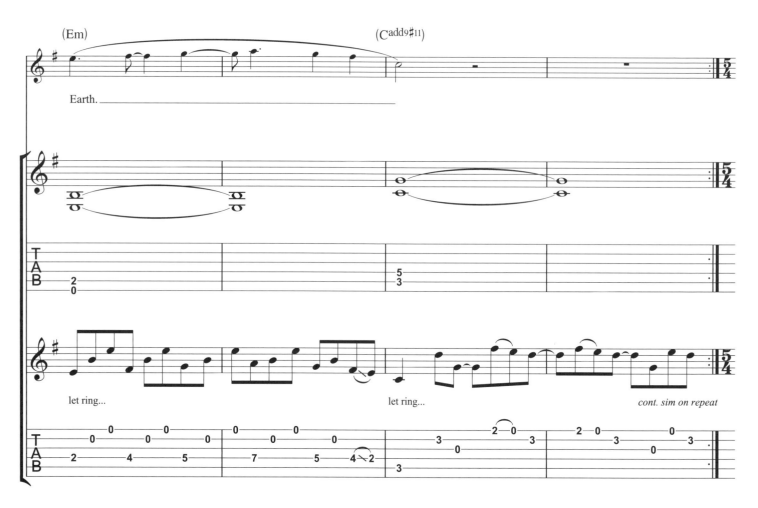

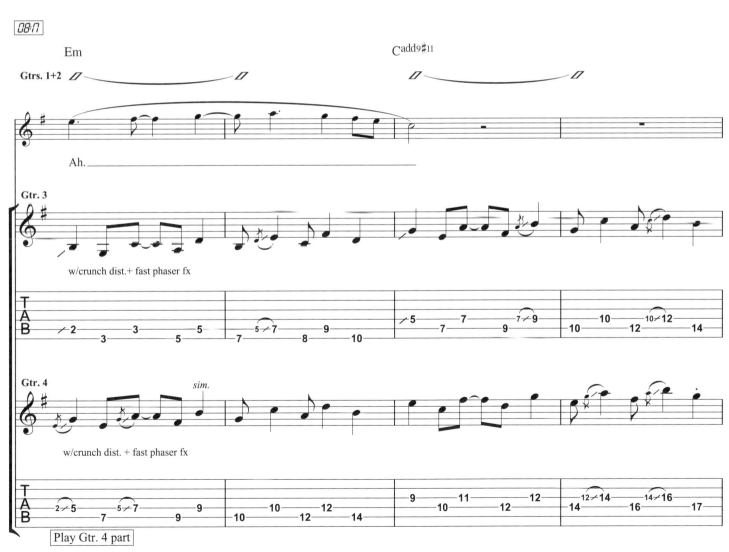

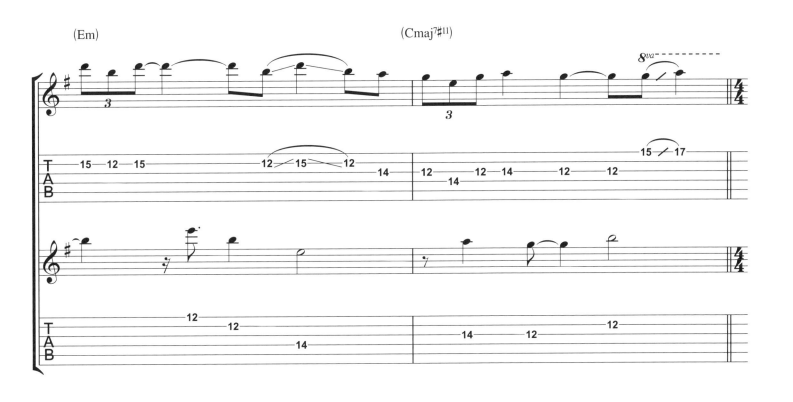
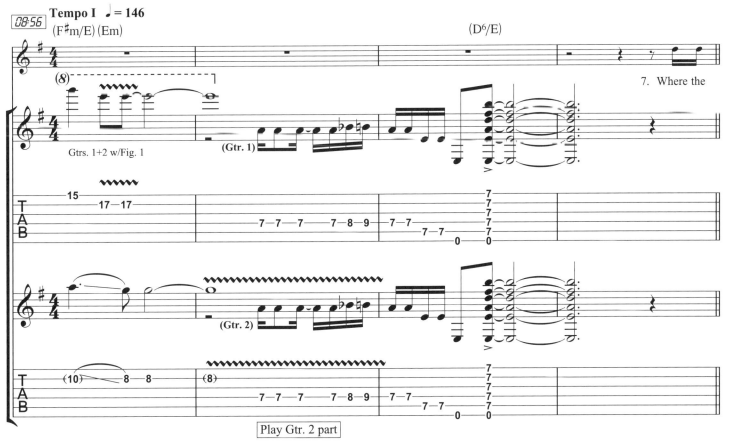

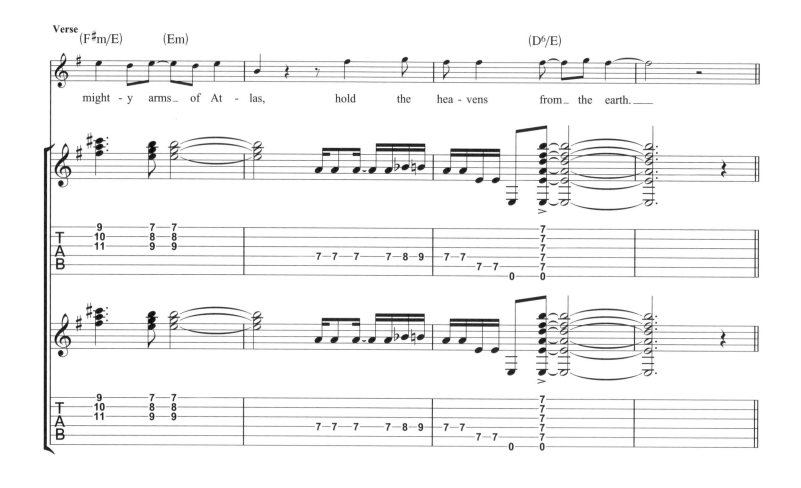
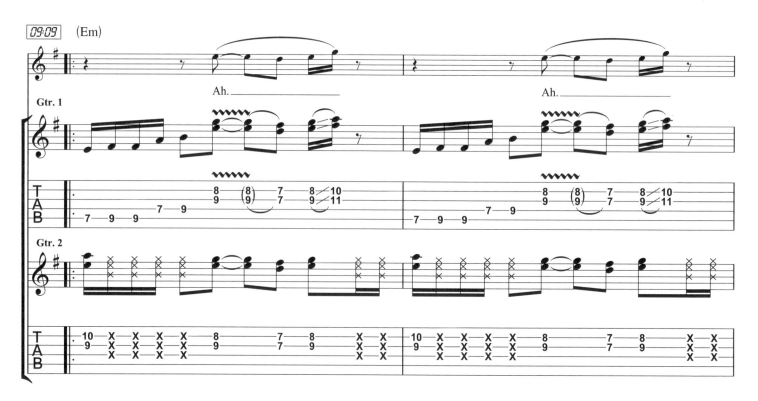

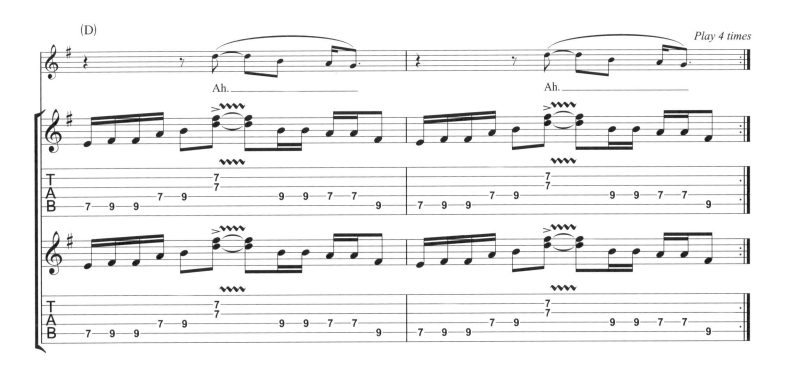
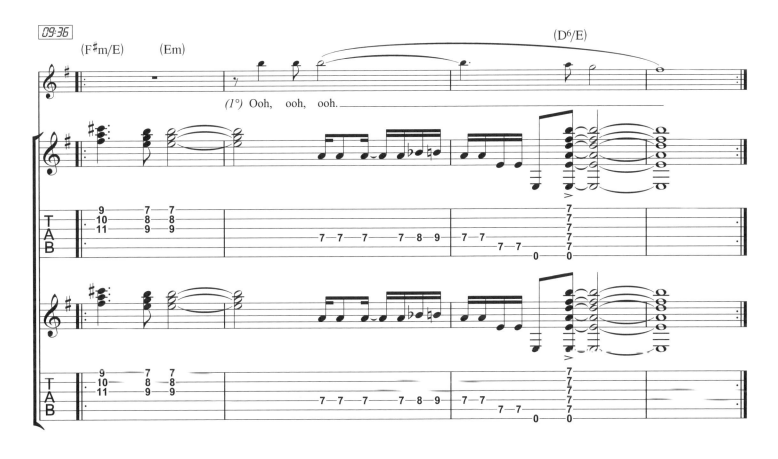
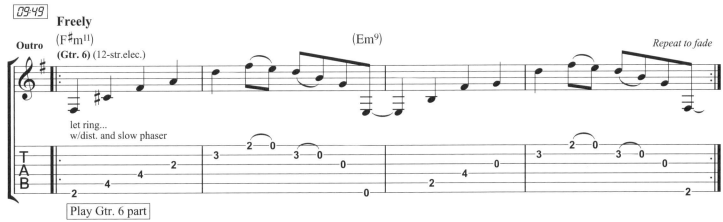

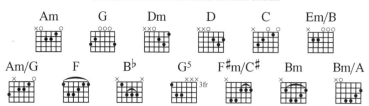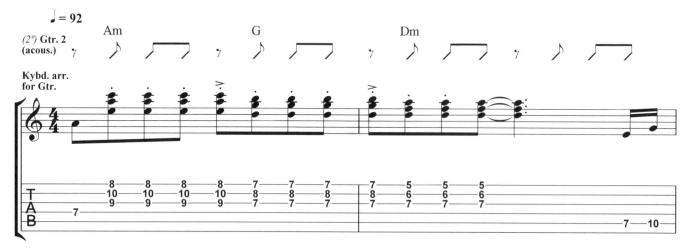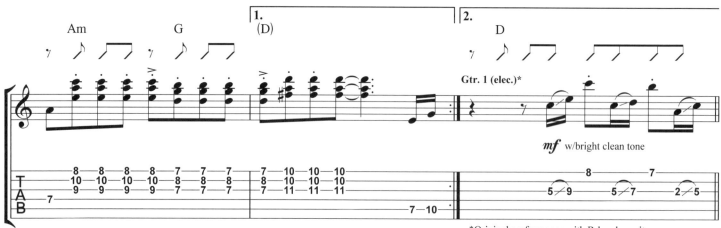

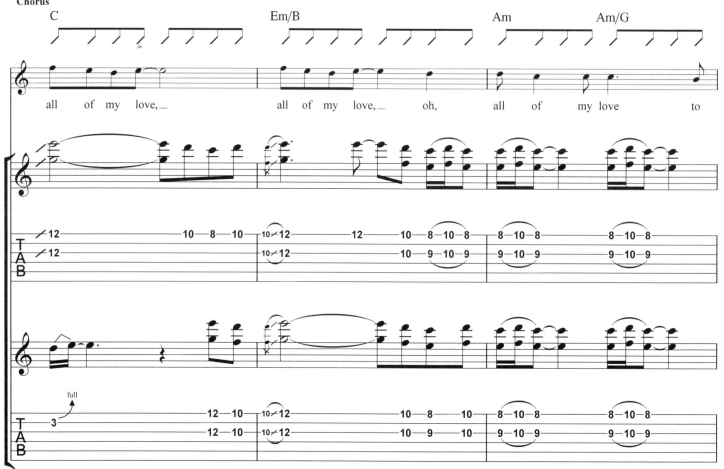

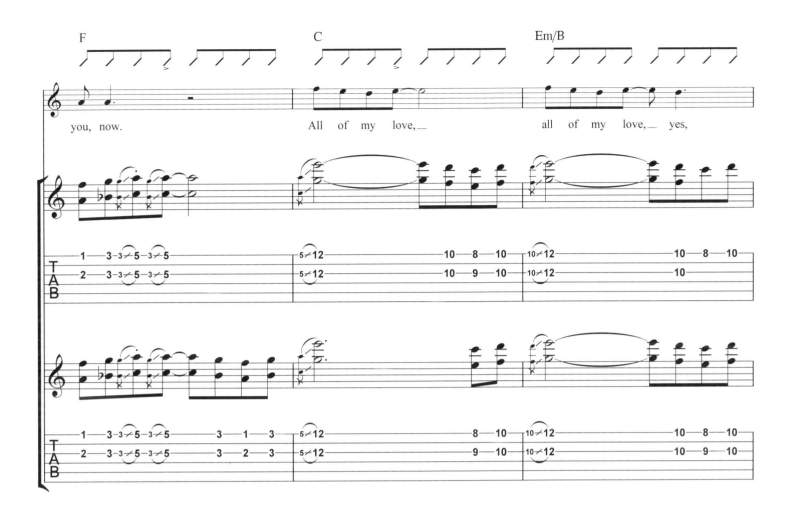

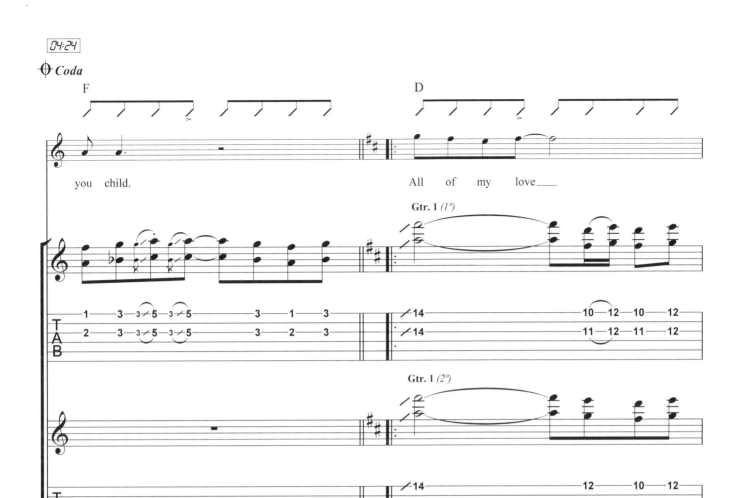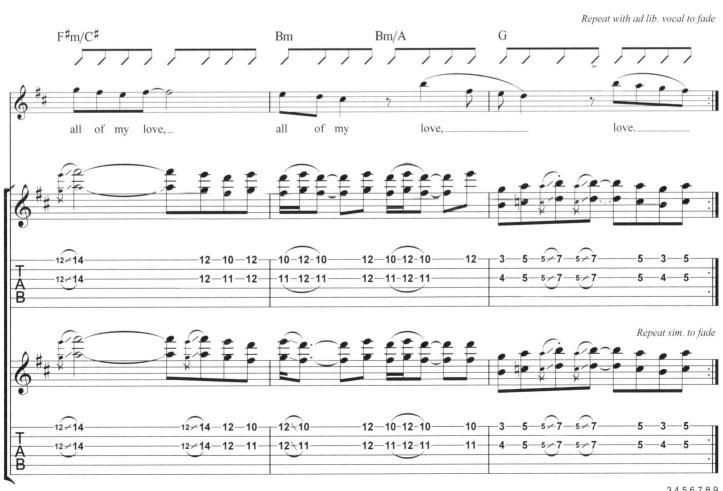

FULL INSTRUMENTAL PERFORMANCES (WITH GUITAR):

DISC 1:

1) Stairway To Heaven
(Page/Plant) Warner/Chappell North America Limited.

2) The Song Remains The Same
(Page/Plant) Warner/Chappell North America Limited.

3) Over The Hills And Far Away
(Page/Plant) Warner/Chappell North America Limited.

4) Trampled Under Foot
(Page/Plant/Jones) Warner/Chappell North America Limited.

5) Kashmir
(Page/Plant/Bonham) Warner/Chappell North America Limited.

6) Nobody's Fault But Mine
(Page/Plant) Warner/Chappell North America Limited.

7) Achilles Last Stand
(Page/Plant) Warner/Chappell North America Limited.

8) All My Love
(Plant/Jones) Warner/Chappell North America Limited.

BACKING TRACKS ONLY (WITHOUT GUITAR):

DISC 2:
1) Stairway To Heaven
2) The Song Remains The Same
3) Over The Hills And Far Away
4) Trampled Under Foot
5) Kashmir
6) Nobody's Fault But Mine
7) Achilles Last Stand
8) All My Love